POND LIFE

Library of Congress Number: 84-26249

Library of Congress Cataloging-in-Publication Data

Kirkpatrick, Rena K.
  Pond life.

  (Look at science)
  Includes index.
  Summary: Easy-to-read text and illustrations explore the plant and animal life in a pond.
  1. Pond ecology—Juvenile literature. [1. Pond ecology. 2. Ecology] I. Title. II. Series.
  QH541.5.P63K57   1985   574.5′26322   84-26249

ISBN 0-8172-2355-X   hardcover library binding

ISBN 0-8114-6901-8   softcover binding

  5 6 7 8 9 10   96 95

POND LIFE

By Rena K. Kirkpatrick
Science Consultant

Illustrated by Annabel Milne and Peter Stebbing

RSVP
RAINTREE
STECK-VAUGHN
P U B L I S H E R S
The Steck-Vaughn Company

Austin, Texas

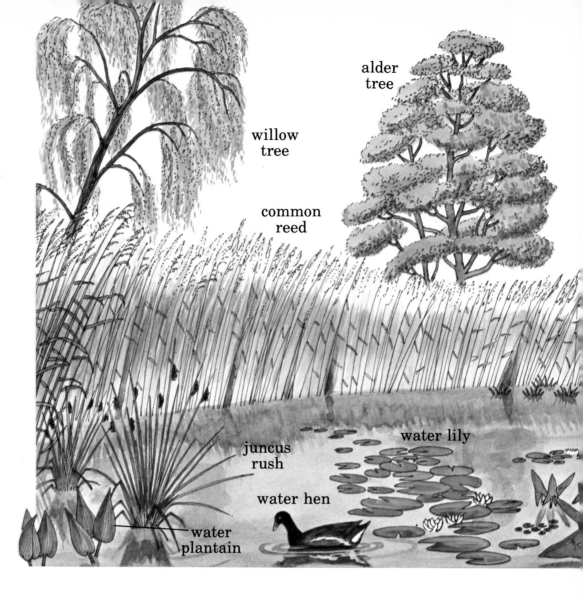

willow tree

alder tree

common reed

juncus rush

water lily

water hen

water plantain

What is life like in a pond?
The plants and animals of a pond live
well together. They are a community.

Where do the plants and animals live?
Some of the plants and animals live
above the water. Others live on and
in the water.

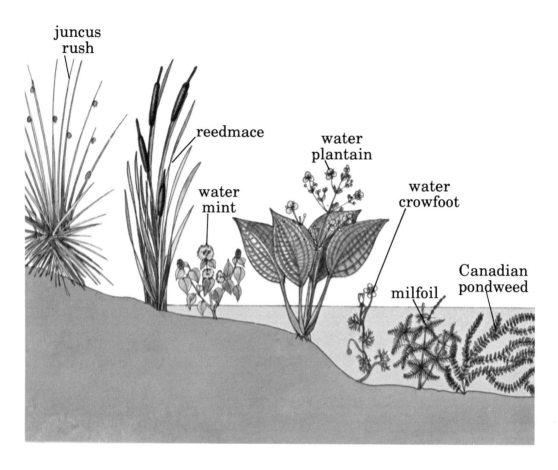

juncus
rush

reedmace

water
mint

water
plantain

water
crowfoot

milfoil

Canadian
pondweed

How do pond plants grow?
Plants that grow near ponds need a
lot of water. Some plants have only
their roots in the water.

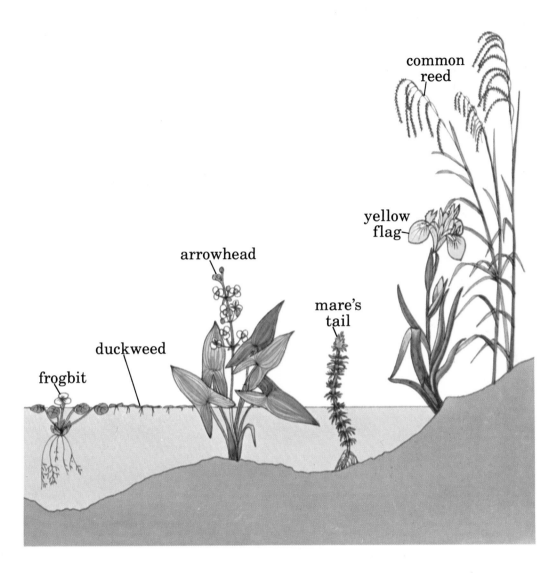

Other plants have roots that float.
Still other plants grow completely
underwater.

water hen

duck

drake

Where do pond birds build nests?
Some of the birds build their nests
on shore. Others build nests in the
middle of the pond.

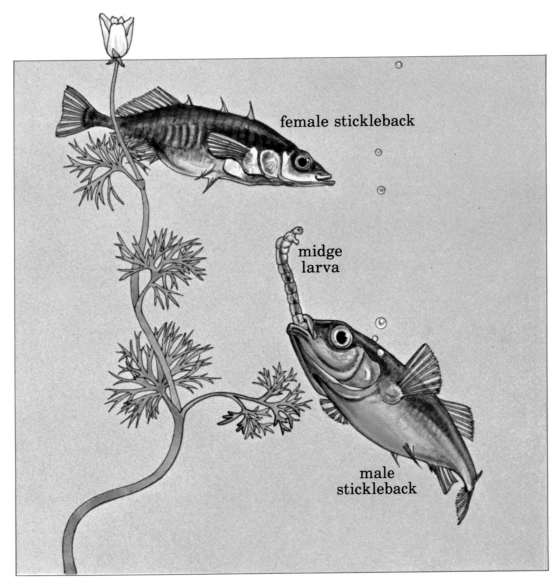

female stickleback

midge
larva

male
stickleback

What are pond fish like?
Many different kinds of fish live in
ponds. Fish eat plants and insects
from the water.

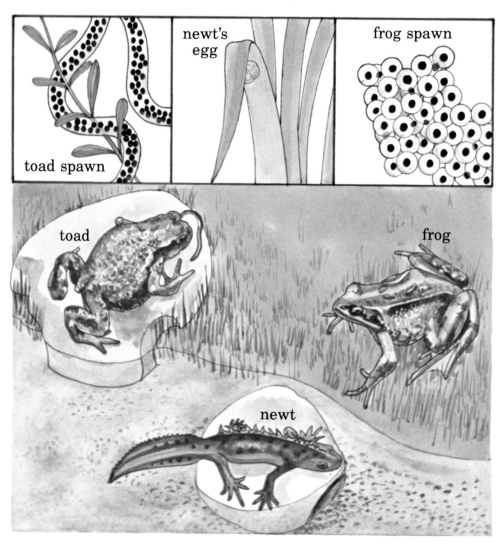

What are some other pond animals?
Frogs, toads, and newts live in water
and on land. Frogs and toads lay eggs
in water. Newts lay eggs in grass.
The young frogs, toads, and newts
live in the water after they hatch.

pondweed

growing tadpoles

What hatches from frog eggs?
Tadpoles hatch from frog eggs.
Tadpoles have tails. They do not
have legs. They eat water plants.

How do tadpoles grow into frogs?
    Tadpoles grow legs as they get older.
They need to eat meat. In the pond,
they eat insects.

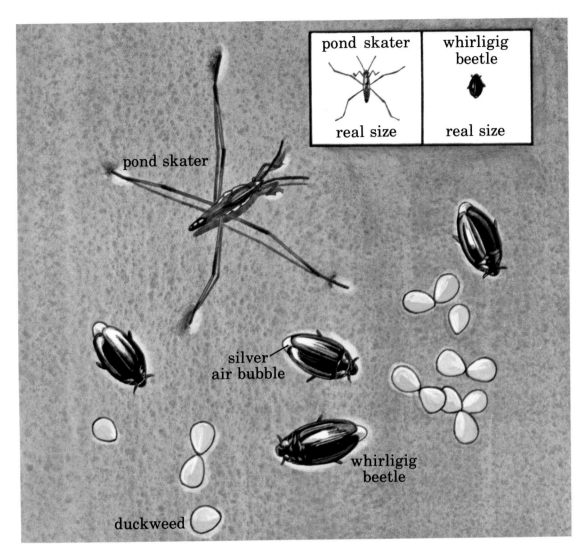

pond skater

whirligig beetle

real size

real size

pond skater

silver
air bubble

whirligig
beetle

duckweed

What are surface insects like?

Some pond insects never go under
the water. They stay on the surface.
Fish, frogs, and birds eat insects as
food.

How a gnat grows

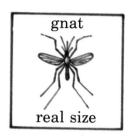
gnat

real size

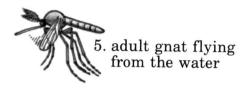
5. adult gnat flying
   from the water

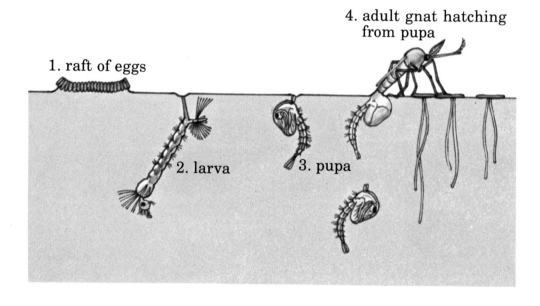
4. adult gnat hatching
   from pupa

1. raft of eggs

2. larva

3. pupa

How do gnats grow in the pond?

Gnats spend most of their lives in the water. Fish eat the eggs, larvae, and pupae of gnats. Frogs eat the adult gnats.

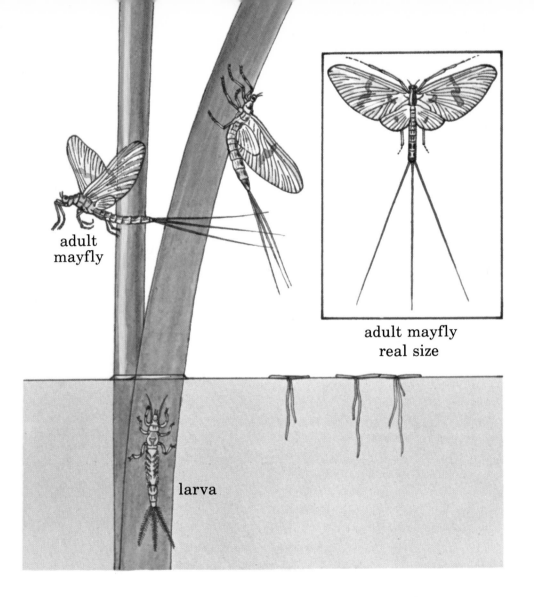

adult
mayfly

adult mayfly
real size

larva

How do mayflies grow in the pond?
The larva of the mayfly lives in the
water for one or two years. The adult
has no mouth, so it cannot eat. Adult
mayflies live for only a few hours.

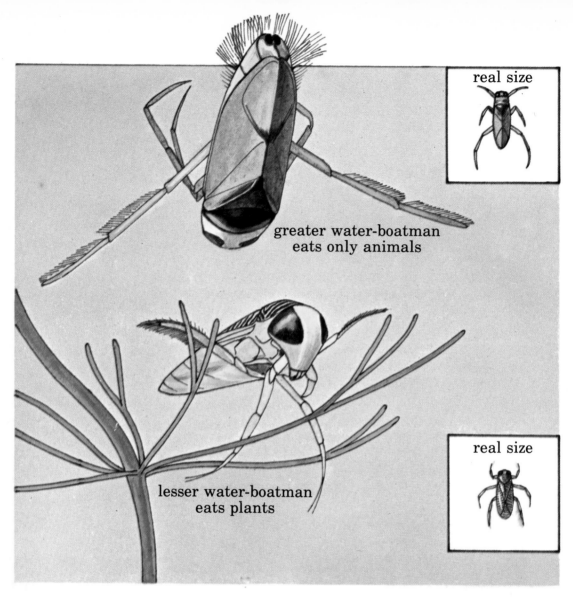

real size

greater water-boatman
eats only animals

lesser water-boatman
eats plants

real size

What other insects live in a pond?
Water-boatmen swim underwater.
They come to the surface for air. One
set of legs acts like oars. Hairs on the
legs push against the water and help
the boatmen swim.

male great
diving beetle

female great
diving beetle

Diving beetles float with their heads
in the water. They trap air under
their wing cases. When they are
underwater, they can breathe the
trapped air for several minutes.

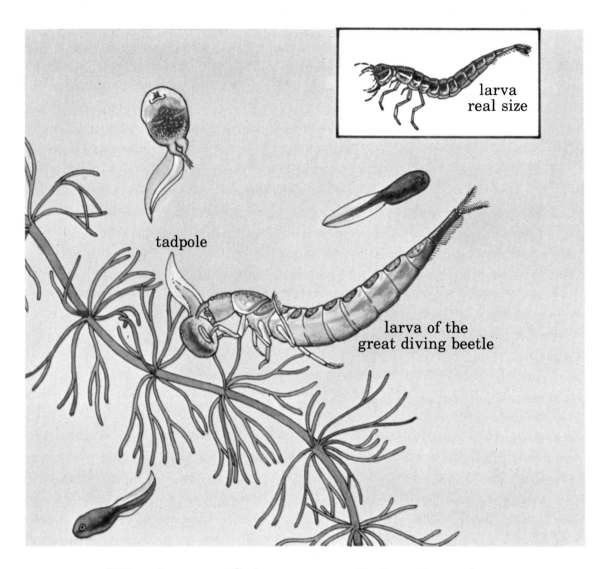

larva
real size

tadpole

larva of the
great diving beetle

The larva of the great diving beetle
attacks and eats many other small
pond animals. It comes to the surface
for air. It traps air with its tail hairs,
which it can breathe for several
minutes.

What can be found on a pond plant?
Just one pond plant has many small
animals on it. Some fall off easily.
Others hold on tightly.

about four times
real size

water
louse

flatworms

What are scavengers?

Flatworms and water lice crawl on
plants at the bottom of the pond.
They eat bits of food left by other
animals. They are called scavengers.

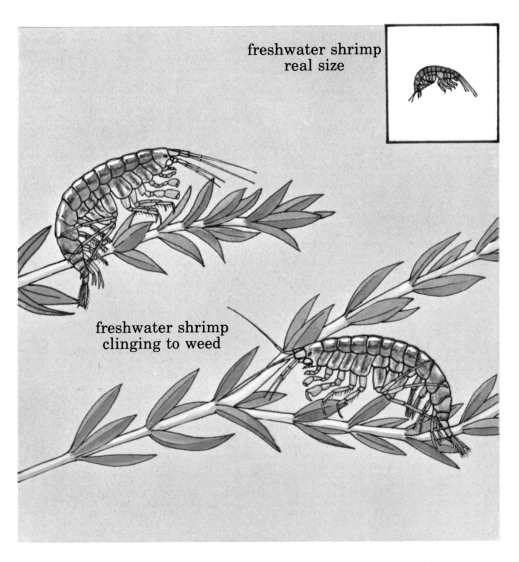

freshwater shrimp
real size

freshwater shrimp
clinging to weed

What other animals live in a pond?
Freshwater shrimp live in ponds.
They have hard shells and many
pairs of legs.

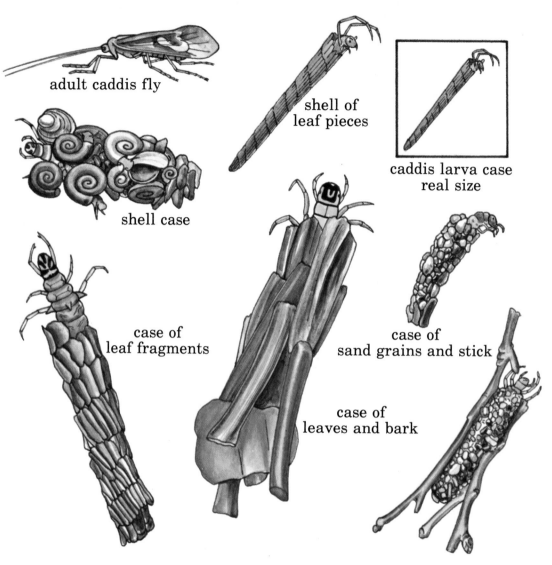

adult caddis fly

shell of
leaf pieces

caddis larva case
real size

shell case

case of
leaf fragments

case of
sand grains and stick

case of
leaves and bark

How do caddis flies grow in a pond?
Caddis flies lay eggs on shore. The
larva returns to the water. Then it
forms a case around itself. The adult
hatches from the case.

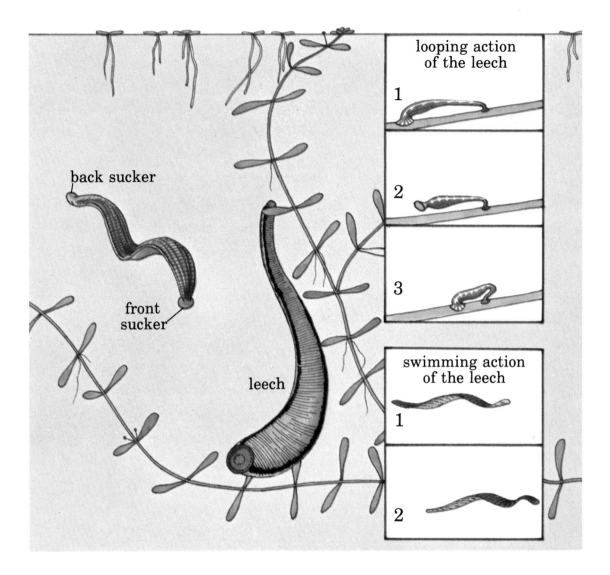

back sucker

front sucker

leech

looping action of the leech

1

2

3

swimming action of the leech

1

2

What are leeches like?

Leeches look like flatworms. They have suckers at each end. Suckers hold onto plants and stones. Leeches are good swimmers.

freshwater winkle

great ramshorn

great pond snail

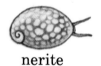

nerite

Jenkin's spire snail

Why do snails have shells?

Shells are the houses of snails. Snails carry their shells with them. Snails have many sizes and shapes.

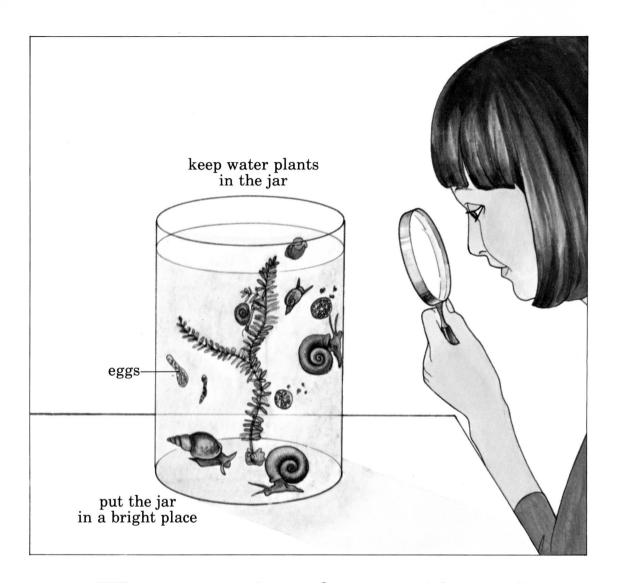

keep water plants
in the jar

eggs—

put the jar
in a bright place

What can you learn from watching snails
with a magnifying glass?

      Snails hatch from eggs. They can
hold on to the side of a glass jar.
Snails are scavengers.

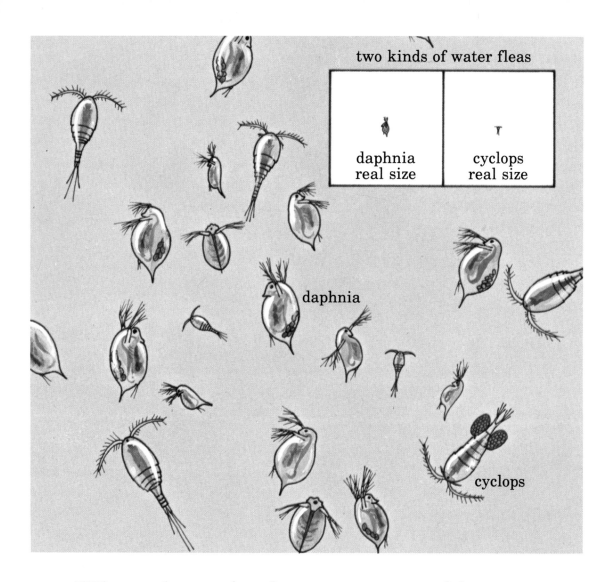

two kinds of water fleas

daphnia real size	cyclops real size

daphnia

cyclops

What other animals can you see with a
magnifying glass?

Water fleas are very small. There are
lots of water fleas in a pond. Other
animals eat them for food.

bucket with
pond water

aquarium tank

wide-necked
jar

waterweed

container

How can you take care of pond animals?
You can keep some pond animals and
plants for only a short time. You
have to be very careful so that they
will live.

leeches

stickleback

great diving
beetle

snails, caddis larvae,
water lice

water-boatman

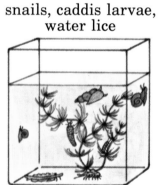

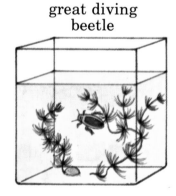

What is the best way to keep animals and plants?

Most animals should be by themselves. Snails, caddis larvae, and water lice will not eat each other. Sticklebacks eat living water fleas.

28

What can you do with the pond animals
and plants?

You can watch them and draw
pictures. You can make a book about
them. After a few days, return the
animals to the pond.

Look at Pond Life Again

Animals and plants of a pond live together in a community.

Pond birds build nests on shore or on the water.

Pond fish eat plants and animals that grow in the pond.

Frogs, toads, and newts lay eggs.

Tadpoles hatch from frog eggs.

Tadpoles grow tails, then legs, and finally turn into frogs.

Some insects live only on the surface of the pond water.

Scavengers eat bits of food left by other animals.

Snail shells are homes for the snails.

A magnifying glass will help you to discover more about pond life.

Look at These Questions About Pond Life

1. Do some pond plants have roots that float?

2. What do pond fish eat?

3. What hatches from frog eggs?

4. How long do mayflies live?

5. How do diving beetles carry air underwater?

6. Where do leeches have suckers?

7. How are snails born?

8. What do sticklebacks eat?

9. How long should you have pond animals away from the pond?

10. Are snails scavengers?

Words in POND LIFE

water
page 5

roots
page 6

surface
page 13

bottom
page 20

case
page 22

sucker
page 23

magnifying
glass
page 25

container
page 27